I HATE Christmas
303 Reasons Why You Should, Too

Crane Hill
PUBLISHERS
BIRMINGHAM, ALABAMA
1996

I HATE Christmas
303 Reasons Why You Should, Too

by Paul Finebaum

(with a little help from the missus)

CRANE HILL
PUBLISHERS

Copyright 1996 by Paul Finebaum

All rights reserved
Printed in the United States of America
Published by Crane Hill Publishers

Library of Congress Cataloging-in-Publication Data

Finebaum, Paul, 1955-
  I hate Christmas: 303 reasons why you should, too / Paul Finebaum (with a little from the missus).
    p.   cm.
  ISBN 1-57587-050-9
  1. Christmas — Psychological aspects. I. Title.
GT4985.F5   1996
394.2'633--dc20   96-19816
                                                                                           CIP

10   9   8   7   6   5   4   3   2   1

I HATE CHRISTMAS

I Hate Christmas Because…

1. Your all-too-perfect sister-in-law has her house decorated just like Martha Stewart's on the day after Thanksgiving—and you can't even remember how many or what color candles to buy for the Advent wreath.

2. The Macy's Thanksgiving Day parade starts the countdown to Christmas, which raises your stress level so high that you can't enjoy your turkey and dressing.

3. You spend the day after Thanksgiving reading all the "How to Reduce Stress and Enjoy the Holidays" articles, and you feel more stressed than ever.

4. You feel even worse after watching the Oprah special on "How to Cope with the Christmas Blues."

5. You keep hearing that to enjoy the holidays you have to take time for yourself.

6. You feel guilty and very selfish when you take time for yourself.

7. It's supposed to be the season of good cheer, but no one ever comes around to cheer YOU up.

8. You decide that for once you're going to take some stress off yourself and not send Christmas cards.

9. But you receive 50 Christmas cards the first day of December and decide to go out and buy some and get them written and mailed in time—causing even more stress than if you had sent them in the first place.

10. While you're trying to find a Christmas card with just the right picture and just the right verse to send THIS year, other people are buying their cards for NEXT year.

11. People send you Christmas cards with family pictures on them.

12. People send you computer printout Christmas letters.

13. You hate reading computer printout Christmas letters, but you know you have to because the people who sent them will call you Christmas Day and you need to know what's in their letter.

14. You wait in line at the post office to buy stamps.

15. You wait in line at the post office to buy more stamps.

16. You wait in line at the post office to mail presents.

17. You wait in line at the post office to mail more presents.

18. No matter how many times you've already waited in line at the post office, you know that you will wait in line at 6 p.m. on December 23rd to overnight cards and presents.

19. As soon as you mail your last Christmas card, you get one from somebody you dropped from your list.

20. You will send Christmas cards to at least seven people who moved the second week of December.

21. People decorate everything in sight.

22. There are green wreaths, twinkling lights, and big red bows on cars and trucks.

23. Doghouses are outlined in colored lights.

24. Dogs sprout fake reindeer antlers.

25. Plastic Santas and Rudolphs stand on front lawns.

26. There's fake snow in every store window—even in Florida and California.

27. Neighbors try to outdo each other decorating their yards.

28. You can count on a blackout at least once a week from too many people having too many outdoor Christmas lights turned on at the same time.

29. People sue each other for using too much electricity for holiday decorations.

30. You want to take your kids to see the Christmas lights, but you can't tear them away away from the VCR and their computer games.

31. There's no escaping the holiday decor.

32. Even toilet paper comes in "festive" Christmas prints.

33. The red and green Christmas message on grocery bags rubs off on your hands and clothes.

34. You can't get the red and green from the grocery bags off your hands and clothes.

35. Poinsettias are ugly.

36. You don't know what do with the poinsettias after Christmas.

37. You carefully tend your Christmas cactus all year–and it blooms the week after New Year's.

38. Artificial Christmas trees are so phony.

39. Real Christmas trees are such a hassle.

40. You want to cut down a tree so you can get a fresh one that's just the right size and shape, but you can't get your spouse or kids to go with you.

41. At the tree lot, you meticulously check every tree before deciding the first one you looked at is the perfect one.

42. When you get the perfect tree home, you find out that it has a huge bare spot and the trunk is crooked.

43. You can't believe you paid $50 for your less-than-perfect tree.

44. You try to make putting up the Christmas tree a special family time, but your spouse and kids all have something else they "absolutely have to do" every day and night the whole month of December.

I HATE CHRISTMAS

45. You have to threaten your kids with bodily harm to get them to help you carry in the tree, wrestle it into the stand, and get it to stand up straight.

46. No matter how carefully you put away the Christmas lights last year, you still have to untangle them this year.

47. You know that if you didn't buy extra Christmas lights when you saw them in the stores in August, you probably won't be able to buy them when you need them.

48. All of the ornaments need to be evenly spaced, and each and every one needs to hang straight.

49. You have to judiciously place your teenage children's first-grade handmade ornaments so they can be seen but aren't obvious.

50. You have to make the treetop angel stand up straight no matter how bent or off-center the top branch is.

51. Every time you walk past your perfectly decorated tree, you stop to "adjust" at least one ornament.

52. Every time anybody walks past your perfectly decorated tree, some of the needles fall off.

53. Your cat climbs your perfectly decorated tree.

54. Your dog "waters" your perfectly decorated tree.

55. Pets and little kids undecorate the lower half of your perfectly decorated tree.

56. You know that taking down your perfectly decorated Christmas tree will be even harder than putting it up.

57. You also know that there's no way you'll ever get every pine needle and every piece of tinsel out of your house.

58. You want to have just one evening at home to sit and admire your perfectly decorated tree.

59. But you won't be able to because you have to go to at least one Christmas party, pageant, or choir concert every night from December 1 to 24.

60. People who look familiar and obviously know all about you come up to you at holiday parties—and you don't have a clue who they are.

61. People hold a sprig of mistletoe over your head and expect to be kissed.

62. At the neighborhood party you have to socialize with people you haven't spoken to all year.

63. You will drink lots of eggnog—and you don't like eggnog unless it's mostly Jack Daniel's.

64. All the other women at holiday parties look thin and glamorous, and you feel fat and frumpy.

65. You swore you would lose enough weight to get into that little black dress by Christmas, but it's tighter than ever.

66. You feel even more fat and frumpy after you watch Richard Simmons's TV program on "How to Lose Weight AFTER the Holidays."

67. You feel downright obese when your mother-in-law says, "Oh, you look great now that you've put on some weight. You used to be too thin!"

68. You can't figure out how to be sociable and sample everyone's special Christmas goodies without gaining 20 pounds before New Year's.

69. Everybody talks about watching calories.

70. Your coworkers bring Christmas cookies and pralines to the office and insist that you "have just one."

71. At least one of your clients will send you flavored popcorn in a Christmas tin, and you won't stop eating it until it's gone.

72. Candy canes taste awful, but you eat them anyway.

73. You see bags and bags of fresh cranberries and wonder once again what the heck they're for and who would ever want to eat them.

74. You decide that it would be fun to string cranberries for the Christmas tree.

75. After three hours of stringing, you end up with nothing but mushed berries and red hands.

76. Everything you eat in December will be made with miniature marshmallows, mayonnaise, Cool Whip, or Velveeta—or all of the above.

77. You will eat red and green Rice Krispies treats.

78. For every raw carrot on the holiday buffet tables, you will eat four pieces of fudge and a piece of German chocolate cake.

79. Someone will serve you year-old fruitcake.

80. You will have to go out and buy Maalox after eating yet another piece of fruitcake–fresh or year-old.

81. You will take at least two extra-strength Advil after you've smiled your way through a conversation with your boss and his wife, who looks like a child bride after her last "nip and tuck" visit to the plastic surgeon.

82. You haven't had a pimple since you were a teenager, but you get a big one right on the tip of your nose the night of the season's biggest holiday party.

83. The office Christmas party is supposed to be the highlight of the working year—but it always turns out to be the most boring event of the working year.

84. People who work together in the same office never have anything to say to each other at the Christmas party.

85. There's never enough liquor at office parties.

86. When you draw names for the office party, you always get the person you like the least.

87. You will spend hours shopping for the "perfect" gift for the office gift exchange.

88. The grab bag at the office party is filled with every kind of worthless gift imaginable.

89. You pick the most worthless gift of all.

90. You suspect that the gift you got at the office party is something that someone had around the house and wanted to get rid of.

91. You not only have to pretend that you like your boss, but you also have to buy your boss a gift.

92. You spend hours shopping for just the right gift for your boss.

93. You wish that your company would give every employee a bigger Christmas bonus instead of spending so much money on a party that no one enjoys.

94. You give each of your employees a Christmas bonus and then overhear them complaining about it not being enough.

95. No work gets done after Thanksgiving because all your employees do is talk about the stress of getting ready for Christmas.

96. Hearing your employees talk about the stress of getting ready for Christmas really stresses you out.

97. Your secretary has a jingle bell necklace, and you'd like to wrap it around her neck.

98. Coworkers start saying, "Merry Christmas!" and sending holiday E-mail the first day back at work after Thanksgiving.

99. The first week of December, people start saying, "Can't this wait until after Christmas?"

100. People also say, "Don't worry–be happy! After all, it's Christmas!"

101. Christmas becomes the universal excuse for letting things slide.

102. Car alarms buzz Christmas music.

103. People leave you Christmas voice mail messages.

104. People send you Christmas greetings on your pager.

105. People put Christmas carols on their answering machines.

106. People wear Christmas ties and sweaters.

107. Christmas sweaters usually smell like mothballs—which is where they've been the last 11 months.

108. Total strangers smile at you and say, "Merry Christmas!" (I hate strangers. If I wanted to talk to strangers, I'd become a talk-show host.)

109. Your mother-in-law makes the same cookies every year and gives you 12 dozen.

110. Nobody ever eats your mother-in-law's cookies—but you don't have the heart to tell her.

111. You have to decide whether to bake or not to bake.

112. There's no way to bake Christmas cookies without eating at least a dozen (raw) and a dozen (baked) from every batch.

113. When it's time to wrap up and give away the holiday goodies you've baked, you find that they've mysteriously disappeared.

114. At least one of your kids will tell you at 9 p.m. one night that you have to send two dozen Christmas cupcakes for the class party the next day.

115. You have to juggle your work schedule so you can attend all of your kids' Christmas programs.

116. You have to explain to your kids that not everyone can play Mary or Joseph—someone has to do the other parts, including being the donkey.

117. For the umpteenth year in a row, you cut up another bathrobe to make a Wise Man's costume and another sheet to make angel wings.

118. You have to explain who Santa Claus is and why he comes on Baby Jesus' birthday.

119. You have to convince your one-year-old that it's okay to sit on Santa's lap.

120. You have to convince your three-year-old that there is a Santa Claus no matter what anybody else says.

121. You have to convince your five-year-old to stop saying there is no Santa Claus.

122. You have to try to explain that there is only one *real* Santa Claus but he has lots of look-alike helpers.

123. You have a harder time explaining why some of Santa's look-alikes are women. (I'm all for equal rights, but isn't this taking things too far?)

124. By the second week of December, all of the Santas need to have their red suits and white beards cleaned— but they don't do it.

125. Some Santas don't pull their "beards" up far enough to cover their dark sideburns.

126. Some street-corner Santas have liquor on their breath.

127. You'd say, "Ho, ho, ho," too if you had to work only one day a year.

128. At least one newspaper columnist dresses up like Santa to do a human interest story. (Come on, fella–go cover a real story instead of the same old pablum.)

129. Your kids wait in line with lots of sniffling, sneezing kids to get a photo with Santa.

130. Photos with Santa cost a fortune.

131. Instead of just sitting on Santa's lap and telling him one or two things they want, some kids bring Santa a nine-page computer printout.

132. You strain to hear what your kids tell Santa so you will buy the right things.

133. You can count on Santa promising to bring your kids at least one item that will be very expensive and in short supply–like a Super Blitzomatic Ninja Power Tron.

134. You take a day off from work and stand in line for nine and a half hours to get one of the precious few Super Blitzomatic Ninja Power Trons in town–and the person in front of you gets the last one.

135. You hope that your kid will stop wanting a Super Blitzomatic Ninja Power Tron by Christmas morning—but no such luck.

136. On Christmas morning you try to explain to your sobbing child that Santa must have run out of Super Blitzomatic Ninja Power Trons, but you're sure he'll bring one next year.

137. Then you have to convince your sobbing child that "next year" isn't really that far away.

138. You also try to convince your sobbing child that being happy doesn't depend on getting a Super Blitzomatic Ninja Power Tron and there are poor children who are happy to get just an orange or an apple for Christmas.

139. No matter what you say, your child still wants a Super Blitzomatic Ninja Power Tron—maybe worse than before.

140. Every Christmas is more commercialized than the last one.

141. The stores stay open all day and all night.

142. The stores are mobbed with people day and night, but newscasters keep warning that "this could be the worst Christmas ever for retailers."

143. You wonder what it would be like if every store closed between Thanksgiving and Christmas.

144. Christmas catalogs start arriving on the Fourth of July.

145. When you call to place an order on the fifth of July, the items you want are out of stock and won't be available until December 26th.

146. No matter how early you start shopping, you still end up rushing out for last-minute gifts on Christmas Eve.

147. If you shop early, the bills will come BEFORE Christmas.

148. You have to take a number and stand in line for at least half an hour at the ATM machine.

149. You worry about how you're going to be able to pay the usual bills, buy groceries, clothe your kids, and have money left over for Christmas.

150. No matter how much money you save or how carefully you budget, you always end up spending too much.

151. Knowing that you don't have the money for Christmas this year, every bank in town tries to get you to open a Christmas fund for NEXT year.

152. How can you start saving for NEXT Christmas when you don't have enough money to pay for THIS Christmas?

153. You promise yourself that you're going to cut back on Christmas spending this year, and you feel guilty when you spend more than you did last year.

154. Starting in October, you are reminded at least twice a day how many more shopping days there are till Christmas.

155. The twice-daily shopping-day countdown ties your stomach into ever-tighter knots.

156. Your wife wants you to take a vacation day the week after Thanksgiving to shop.

157. Your wife will be unhappy if you don't take a vacation day to shop.

158. You'll be unhappy if you do take a vacation day to shop.

159. No matter when you go shopping, you will spend 35 minutes getting off the ramp of the interstate near the mall and another 35 minutes looking for a parking place.

160. The entire time you're trying to find a parking place, your wife will keep saying, "We should have come shopping last Saturday instead of going to that stupid football game."

161. You can buy everything but the one thing you really need—a parking place.

162. Manufacturers and merchandisers prey on Christmas shoppers.

163. You know they'll come out with a new Windows program—just in time for Christmas.

164. One mail-order company sells Panty Claus—the perfect stocking stuffer.

165. Every year would-be authors come out with gimmicky books sold ONLY at Christmastime.

166. First there was *The Cajun Night Before Christmas.*

167. Now there's *The Redneck Night Before Christmas.*

168. You spend hours shopping for the perfect gift for each of your out-of-state nieces and nephews and end up getting each of them yet another pair of gloves.

169. You spend hours shopping for a gift your grandfather will really enjoy and end up buying him yet another bottle of Old Spice.

170. You spend hours shopping for a gift your grandmother will really enjoy and end up buying her yet another lilac-scented sachet.

171. Christmas sweatshirts come only in "One Size Fits All"–and you know your wife doesn't wear the same size Dolly Parton does.

172. Ten of the worst Christmas gift ideas ever are: The Snoop Doggy Dogg Christmas CD.

173. The remake of *The Miracle on 34th Street* starring Michael Jackson as Kris Kringle.

174. *A Merry Christmas in Under 10 Minutes* starring Divine Brown.

175. *The Baywatch Christmas Special.*

176. Kathie Lee Gifford's personal line of fruitcakes.

177. *The O. J. Simpson Family Christmas Special.*

178. *My Favorite Christmas Stories* by the Unabomber.

179. *Home for the Holidays* starring Howard Stern.

180. *How to Lose Weight and Have More Sex During the 12 Days of Christmas* by Ricki Lake.

181. The latest Elvis Christmas CD featuring "Blue Christmas."

182. No matter how many times you make a list and check it twice, you will wake up in the middle of the night thinking about someone you forgot.

183. You have to make sure you give the same number of gifts to each of your kids because they will count them on Christmas morning.

184. You also have to make sure you spend the same amount of money on each of your kids because they will know if you don't.

185. You want to buy matching sweatshirts for all three of your kids, but the store will have only two in the right sizes.

186. Wrapping paper costs as much as a nice gift.

187. You either spend half an hour picking the right paper and carefully wrapping each package yourself or you wait in line at the Christmas gift-wrapping counter.

188. If you leave your gifts at the counter to be wrapped while you do some more shopping, you might forget you left them there.

189. If you forget to pick up your packages, you have to go back to the gift-wrapping counter and try to get back what is rightfully yours.

190. You might get so frustrated at yourself and the store clerk that you want to scream, but then you'd have to come up with something good to tell the security guard who comes to arrest you.

191. You have to find boxes big enough to camouflage the gifts your kids know they're getting.

192. You have to hide the gifts where your kids won't find them.

193. Your kids already know all the good hiding places in the house.

194. There's a good chance that you'll hide a few of the gifts so well that neither you nor your kids will find them until long after Christmas.

195. Almost every toy or gadget you buy for your kids says "Batteries Not Included."

196. You spend a small fortune on batteries for all the toys and gadgets you bought that say "Batteries Not Included."

197. Every checkout clerk automatically asks, "Do you need batteries?"

198. Energizer ads constantly remind you "don't forget the batteries," and for once you wish the Bunny would just stop going.

199. You wonder if we're celebrating the birth of the Energizer Bunny.

200. You spend a small fortune on stocking stuffers.

201. You wrap up socks, socks, and more socks.

202. You have to buy or make just the right gift for each of your kids' teachers.

203. You have to buy just the right under-$2 gifts for each of your kids' classroom parties.

204. You feel slightly uncomfortable around your Jewish, Islamic, and Buddhist friends and want to do something special for them.

205. You give your Jewish, Islamic, and Buddhist friends Christmas presents—which makes them feel slightly uncomfortable.

206. Sometimes when you get back to your car after Christmas shopping, you just cry uncontrollably.

207. You get a Christmas note from your paperboy thanking you for your business and reminding you that he is paying his way through college and greatly appreciates tips.

208. You give the mailman a tip, and you don't even know his name.

209. You hear about carolers coming to other people's houses, but they never come to yours.

210. You want to go caroling, but you can't find anyone who will go with you.

211. When you go to the mall in August you hear "It's Beginning to Look a Lot like Christmas."

212. Before the Christmas season is over, you will have heard "Grandma Got Run Over by a Reindeer" at least a billion times.

213. You will also hear dogs barking "Jingle Bells," but you won't hear a Madonna song anywhere.

214. No matter how many times you hear *The Twelve Days of Christmas,* you can't remember all the words—but someone you know will, and they'll insist on singing and acting out the whole thing.

215. Radio stations promise 24 hours of nonstop Christmas music on Christmas Eve—and advertise it every 5 minutes for 24 days ahead of time.

216. The 10 worst Christmas songs ever written are: "Jingle Bell Rock."

217. "A Chipmunk Christmas."

218. "All I Want for Christmas Is My Two Front Teeth."

219. "Deck the Halls."

220. "Here We Go A-Wassailing."

221. "I Saw Mommy Kissing Santa Claus."

222. "Rockin' Around the Christmas Tree."

223. "Have a Holly, Jolly Christmas."

224. "Blue Christmas."

225. "Grandma Got Run Over by a Reindeer."

226. The Budweiser frogs sing and dance to "Jingle Bells."

227. Dennis Rodman dyes his hair green and wears a red Santa cap.

228. Television newscasters talk about "I'm Dreaming of a White Christmas" on Pearl Harbor Day.

229. Some people protest that "I'm Dreaming of a White Christmas" is a racist song.

230. Some people protest that having Nativity scenes on the lawn of city hall is a violation of the separation of church and state.

231. Other people take out ads to remind you to "keep Christ in Christmas."

232. You see countless commercials for the annual Dolly Parton Christmas special. (There are only two things special about Dolly, and neither one has anything to do with Christmas.)

233. No one the least bit interesting ever has a TV Christmas special.

234. You wish they'd stop running *The Charlie Brown Christmas Special.* (That kid is the biggest whiner ever.)

235. As much as you like Jimmy Stewart, you wish *It's a Wonderful Life* wouldn't be shown 23,000 times between Thanksgiving and Christmas.

236. You watch *The Miracle on 34th Street* and know that the only miracle that ever occurred on 34th Street was not getting mugged.

237. If they made *The Miracle on 34th Street* today, it would ruin the actors' careers.

238. Ten movies that will help you hate Christmas even more are (yes, these are real movies): *Silent Night, Bloody Night.*

239. *Ernest Saves Christmas.*

240. *The Nightmare Before Christmas.*

241. *National Lampoon's Christmas Vacation.*

242. *Toys.*

243. *The Christmas Wife.*

244. *Home Alone 2: Lost in New York.*

245. *Bush Christmas.*

246. *Black Christmas.*

247. *Santa Claus Conquers the Martians.*

248. Your in-laws' Christmas traditions are so different from your family's.

249. You drive 15 miles per hour in hopes of being the last one to get to your in-laws' for Christmas Eve dinner so you won't have to think of things to talk about with them.

250. Your brother-in-law drives even slower than you do, though, and you have to converse with your in-laws until he gets there.

251. On Christmas Eve, the local weatherman breaks in with a special update every half hour and keeps pointing out something "mysterious" on the radar screen.

252. You make sure you buy and wrap everything your kids have asked for and even just thought of, and at 8 p.m. Christmas Eve they see a commercial for something they REALLY want.

253. You know that at 2 a.m. Christmas morning you'll be putting together a German bicycle imported through a Japanese wholesaler complete with Chinese instructions.

254. You get to bed about 4 a.m., and at 5 a.m. your kids jump on your bed and wake you up to tell you that Santa has brought a million presents.

255. You try to convince your kids that 5 a.m. is too early to get up even if it is Christmas and Santa has brought a million presents.

256. On Christmas morning the paper will be ripped off packages you spent half an hour each wrapping.

257. You feel guilty about throwing out used but still usable wrapping paper.

258. But there's no use saving the paper because you'll feel guilty if you wrap another present in it.

259. You also feel guilty about throwing out used bows.

260. You have to keep reminding yourself that you can buy 100 brand-new bows for $5.

261. Your spouse surprises you with that special gift only to find out that it's NOT what you have been wanting for the last 51 weeks and 6 days.

262. When she realizes your disappointment, you try to convince her how special it really is—which gives you a Super Bowl-size headache.

263. You give your wife a gift certificate, and she immediately goes out and exchanges it for bigger size.

264. Your husband gives you a Wonder Bra.

265. Your kids give you cologne that makes you gag, but you have to say, "Oh, what a great smell."

266. Your in-laws have never given you anything you wanted or liked.

267. You feel sad when your mom and dad can't remember the next day what you gave them for Christmas.

268. You feel guilty when you stick the clothing your parents gave you in the back of your closet.

269. You'll also feel guilty when you wear the clothing your parents gave you only when they come to visit.

270. A friend's kid gives you a pitying look when he opens your gift and you both realize he's at least five years too old for it.

271. You give your kids every "hot" toy known to man and they complain five minutes after they open the last package that there's nothing to do.

272. You spend all day cooking Christmas turkey dinner and the kids beg to go to McDonald's for a Happy Meal.

273. You want your husband to help clean up after Christmas dinner, but he's already fallen asleep in his chair.

274. On the sixth day of Christmas, you have to come up with yet another recipe for leftover turkey.

275. You want to spend some nice, quiet, romantic time alone with your wife, but every time you make your move on her, the doorbell or phone rings.

276. You feel grumpier by the moment.

277. Speaking of the moment, it's lost for another Christmas.

278. You have to either visit or entertain all of your in-town relatives on Christmas Day so no one feels slighted.

279. You feel guilty about experiencing a surge of cheer and goodwill AFTER all of your relatives leave.

280. Out-of-town relatives you haven't talked to in a year will call and scream, "Merry Christmas," and you won't even remember their names.

281. Aunt Susie calls, and you have to bribe your kids into sounding grateful for the gloves she sent them.

282. You want to watch a great football game Christmas afternoon, but all that's on is the Blue-Gray game. (If those players were any good, they'd be playing on New Year's Day.)

283. Some people feel so alone at Christmastime, and it only makes them feel worse when you ask, "What are you doing for the holidays?"

284. When you go next door to give your elderly neighbor the preserves you made for her, you spot the preserves you gave her the past two Christmases sitting unopened on her pantry shelf.

285. You always have to go out the week after Christmas and buy yourself what you really wanted–if you can still afford it and if it is still available.

286. The after-Christmas sales start at the crack of dawn December 26th.

287. It's impossible to find a parking place the day after Christmas.

288. The stores are more crowded than ever the day after Christmas.

289. Shoppers have lost their holiday spirit and turn ugly the day after Christmas.

290. Store clerks are at their wit's end the day after Christmas.

291. You spend a whole day waiting in lines to return or exchange Christmas gifts.

292. You hate to go back to work after Christmas because you have to deal with all the things you decided could "wait until after Christmas."

293. Nothing gets done at the office the week between Christmas and New Year's because all of your clients' offices are closed for the holidays.

294. Coworkers bring their leftover Christmas goodies to the office because they're "counting calories."

295. There are traditionally 12 days of Christmas, but since it took God only 6 days to create Heaven and Earth, surely we can cut down on the number of days for this holiday.

296. After Christmas comes New Year's, and I hate New Year's even more than Christmas.

297. Dead Christmas trees line the streets the day after New Year's.

298. After all the buildup, it's depressing when the holidays are finally over.

299. Christmas is the one day of the year you really wouldn't mind it snowing, but it never does.

300. The snow you hoped for on Christmas finally comes while you're at work January 2nd, and you get stuck in a snowbank on the way home.

301. People try to take advantage of totally frustrated Christmas shoppers with books like this.

302. On January 1st, there are only 356 more shopping days until Christmas.

303. You want Christmas to be the way it was when you were a kid—and you'll feel sad because it isn't.